D1137942

the Girls' Summer book

Buster Books

Written by Ellen Bailey
Illustrated by Lisa Jackson
Edited by Hannah Cohen
Designed by Zoe Quayle

Cover illustrated by Nikalas Catlow
With special thanks to Hannah Thornton

The publisher and authors disclaim, as far as is legally permissible, all liability for accidents, or injuries, or loss that may occur as a result of information of instructions given in this book. Use your best common sense at all times — always wear appropriate safety gear, be very careful with scissors, stay within the law and local rules, and be considerate of other people.

First published in Great Britain in 2010 by Buster Books,
an imprint of Michael O'Mara Books Limited,
9 Lion Yard, Tremadoc Road, London SW4 7NQ

Copyright © Buster Books 2010

All rights reserved. No part of this book may be reproduced, stored in a retrieval system, or transmitted in any form or by any means, without the prior permission in writing of the publisher, nor be otherwise circulated in any form of binding or cover other than that in which it is published and without a similar condition including this condition being imposed on the subsequent purchase.

A CIP catalogue record for this book is available from the British Library.

ISBN: 978-1-906082-80-2

2 4 6 8 10 9 7 5 3 1

www.mombooks.com/busterbooks

This book was printed in March 2010 at L.E.G.O., Viale dell'Industria 2, 36100, Vicenza, Italy.

CONTENTS

Design a crown and a necklace of flowers
for the Queen of Summer.

SUMMER SNAPS

Can you work out which girl took each of the photos below
at the summer garden party?

You'll need to think about where each photographer is standing, and which girl she
is aiming her camera at. Check your answers on page 62.

BREAKFAST IN BED

What better way to celebrate summer than with a delicious breakfast in bed served on a beautiful home-made tray?

You can make breakfast for yourself and take it back to bed, or treat your parents to a beautiful breakfast surprise.

A TRAY FOR YOUR TREATS

Follow the instructions below to find out how to make a pretty breakfast tray to present your tasty treats on.

You will need:

• an old wooden tray (check it's okay to use first) • a selection of old magazines • brightly coloured acrylic paints • paintbrushes • PVA glue

1. Paint a thick layer of brightly coloured paint on both the inside and the outside surfaces of the tray. Leave the tray to dry completely.

2. Look through your magazines, and cut out any pictures that you think will look good on your tray – a selection of summery flowers is perfect.

3. Arrange the pictures on the middle of the tray and move them around until you are happy with how they look.

4. Stick your pictures on to the tray using PVA glue.

5. Using a large paintbrush, cover the whole of the tray with PVA glue. This will fix your pictures in place and give the tray a shiny, professional finish. Don't forget to cover the painted areas too.

6. Leave the tray to dry overnight before using it.

BREAKFAST PERFECTION

When you wake up in the morning, follow the steps below
to prepare a brilliant brekkie.

1. Pour a glass of your favourite fruit juice and add a couple of ice cubes.

2. Choose your favourite breakfast food to serve as the main dish. Cereals should be served already poured out into the bowl, with a small jug of milk by the side. Bread, toast or croissants should be served on a pretty plate with a small dish of butter or other spread, and perhaps some jam by the side.

3. Make a fruit salad by chopping lots of different types of fruit into bite-sized pieces. (Ask an adult to help you when chopping fruit with knives.) Mix the fruit together in a bowl with a cup of your favourite fruit juice – the acid in the juice will stop the fruit turning brown in the bowl.

4. Fold a napkin or a paper towel in half to form a triangle and place it in the corner of your home-made tray.

5. Present the rest of your breakfast neatly on the tray. Pop all the cutlery you will need on top of the napkin.

Top Tip. For an extra-special touch, fill a small vase with flowers and place it in the top right-hand corner of the tray.

DID YOU KNOW?

A 'fast' is a long period of time without eating – so 'breakfast' means breaking the fast you've been on since the night before.

TOP-TO-TOE SUMMER BEAUTY

Whether you're heading off to the beach on your summer holidays or spending it at home, get ready to shine with these make-and-use summer beauty products.

HEALING HAIR WRAP

Sunshine, sea water and chlorine can all dry out your hair and leave it looking dull and straw-like, so try out this moisturizing conditioning treatment to restore shine.

First, warm a towel on a radiator or in a tumble-dryer. Next, wash your hair and slick a thick layer of conditioner on it before wrapping it in the hot towel. Leave for ten minutes. During this time use a hairdryer to warm your hair through the towel. Rinse, dry, and then show off your gorgeous silky locks!

HEAVENLY HONEY AND OATMEAL FACE MASK

Soothe sun-kissed skin with this cooling face mask. Mix one tablespoon of natural yogurt with one tablespoon of porridge oats and a few drops of honey.

Apply a thick layer to your face, avoiding the skin around your eyes, and leave for ten minutes. Rinse with warm water then apply a thick layer of moisturizer. Your face will now feel soothed and ready for another day in the sun.

SWEET SKIN BODY SCRUB

Relieve dry skin and remove dead skin cells with this delicious body scrub.

Pour two tablespoons of caster sugar into a bowl. Add the juice of half a lemon and four tablespoons of olive oil. Massage the mixture into your skin, then rinse off in a warm bath before bedtime. Pat your skin dry before getting into bed.

When you wake up in the morning, the remaining olive oil on your skin will have soaked in, making your skin feel sumptuously smooth.

GLITTER LIPGLOSS

You can dazzle on a summer's day simply by adding a flash of glitter. Find an old lipstick and scoop out the leftover colour into a bowl. Add some petroleum jelly and some craft glitter. Leave in the sunshine until it starts to melt.

Using a metal teaspoon, blend the mixture together. Scoop the mixture into the old lipstick case then place in the fridge to set. After one hour, dab some on your lips to complete your sparkly summer style.

REFRESHING LIME AND MINT FOOT SOAK

Walking around barefoot or in sandals can cause the skin on your feet to become rough. To soften up your feet, prepare a refreshing foot soak by putting ten mint leaves in a large bowl.

Chop a lime into quarters (ask an adult to help you with this), add to the bowl and use the back of a spoon to crush everything together.

Fill a clean washing-up bowl with warm water and add the limes and mint mixture. Soak your feet for 15 minutes until soothed and refreshed. Pat them dry with a clean towel and apply moisturizer. Your feet will now feel soft and smooth again.

WHICH SUMMER GODDESS ARE YOU?

Follow this funky flowchart to find out.

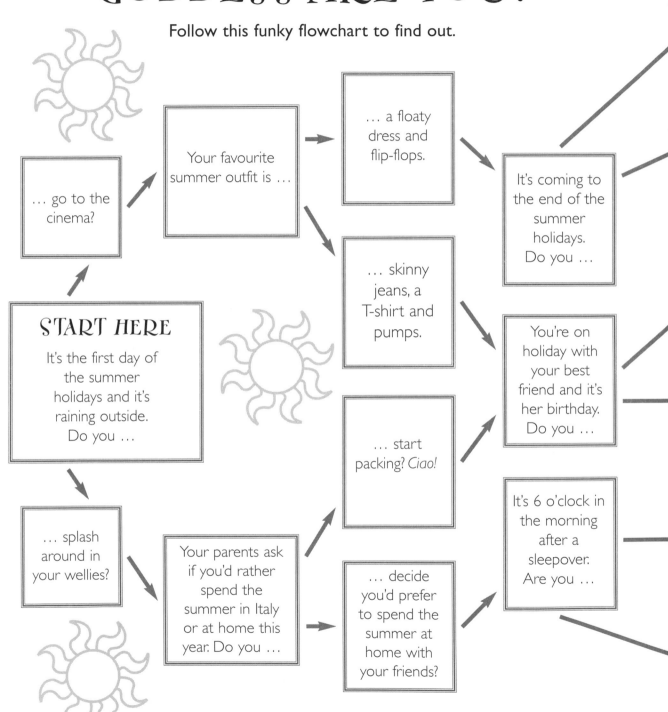

... go to the cinema?

Your favourite summer outfit is ...

... a floaty dress and flip-flops.

It's coming to the end of the summer holidays. Do you ...

START HERE

It's the first day of the summer holidays and it's raining outside. Do you ...

... skinny jeans, a T-shirt and pumps.

You're on holiday with your best friend and it's her birthday. Do you ...

... splash around in your wellies?

Your parents ask if you'd rather spend the summer in Italy or at home this year. Do you ...

... start packing? *Ciao!*

... decide you'd prefer to spend the summer at home with your friends?

It's 6 o'clock in the morning after a sleepover. Are you ...

... make the most of relaxing in your back garden?

... try to pack in as many fun activities as possible?

... plan to go to a theme park she's been talking about?

... invite all the holiday-makers over for a fancy-dress party?

... already getting ready for a fun-filled day?

... tired because you stayed up talking most of the night before?

YOU ARE HEMERA, GODDESS OF SUNSHINE

You love the long summer days and adore playing outside in the sunshine. Complete your goddess look with a sun-shaped hair clip and a yellow ribbon.

YOU ARE AESTAS, GODDESS OF SUMMER

You're bursting with energy. Your friends love that you're full of exciting ideas of things to do and places to visit. Complete your goddess look by pinning plaits of grass into your hair.

YOU ARE IRIS, GODDESS OF RAINBOWS

You love to travel and the summer holidays give you the chance to visit new places and meet new people. Make a necklace of rainbow-coloured beads to complete your goddess look.

YOU ARE ANTHEIA, GODDESS OF FLOWERS

You are a chilled-out girl who likes spending time at home with your friends over the summer holidays. You appreciate the beauty of summer. Pin some fresh flowers in your hair to complete your goddess look.

STEP IT UP FOR SUMMER

When the sun is shining and you feel like dancing, why not make up your very own summer street-dance routine?

POP ON YOUR DANCING SHOES

To get started, slip on some loose clothes – tracksuit bottoms, a T-shirt and your favourite trainers are ideal. Take a portable music player outside and turn on your favourite dance track. Now you are ready to have a go at these sassy street-dance moves. You can create your own cool routine by mixing up the moves below, in whichever order you choose. Once you've got the hang of it, why not have a competition with your friends and battle it out to see who's got the best moves? You can even throw your own signature street-dance move in to the mix!

Dime Stop

Wave 1

Wave 2

Dance around, then suddenly stop. Wait two beats, then continue dancing.

Move your whole body as if a wave of motion is passing through you. This move looks really good if you do it with a friend. Stretch your arms out to either side and make the wave travel from fingertip to fingertip, as above.

The Robot

Dance using stiff, precise movements – as if you're a robot.

The Swag

Sway your arms in time to the music, while walking on the spot.

Drop It

With your hands above your head, bend your knees and drop all the way to the floor, then 'pop' back up without pausing.

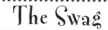

Pop-Lock Walk

Imagine your arms and legs are connected with string so that when you lift your right arm up your right leg also lifts and vice versa.

Heel-Toe Flick

Bend your knees and turn your feet out so that your heels are facing each other. On the next beat of the music, turn your feet in so the toes are now facing each other. Repeat.

Running Girl

Run on the spot while bending your arms up to your chest. As you run, straighten your arms out in front of you in time to the music.

13

IT'S CAKE O'CLOCK!

Sunny summer days are the best time to throw an afternoon tea party. Read on to learn how to throw the perfect party.

CUTE CUPCAKES

Cute cupcakes are great tea-party food. Here's how to bake up a batch:

You will need:

For the cakes: • 2 eggs • 100 g caster sugar • 100 g self-raising flour • 100 g butter • 18 to 20 cupcake cases **For the icing:** • 100 g icing sugar • 50 g butter • glace cherries, chocolate buttons, sprinkles etc.

1. Turn the oven on to Gas Mark 4/ 180 °C.

2. Place the cake ingredients into a large mixing bowl and stir with a wooden spoon until you have a smooth mixture.

3. Arrange your cupcake cases over two bun tins – this mixture makes 18 to 20

cupcakes. Put two teaspoons of mixture into each case.

4. Ask an adult to bake the cakes in the oven for 10 to 15 minutes, or until they are golden brown on top.

5. Ask an adult to help you take the cakes out of the oven and place them on a wire rack to cool.

6. Put the icing sugar and butter into a bowl and stir until smooth.

7. Use a knife to spread the icing on the top of each cupcake. Decorate with cherries, chocolate buttons or whatever you like!

CAKE STAND PERFECTION

To add a touch of elegant sophistication to your tea party, why not make a cake stand to present your cute cupcakes on? Here's how:

You will need:

• 3 party cups (paper or plastic) • a sharp pencil • a blob of modelling clay • 3 m of gift ribbon • scissors • 2 small party plates • 1 paper party plate • sticky tape

1. Position a cup on top of the modelling clay. Push the tip of the pencil through the middle of the cup base into the clay to make a small hole.

2. Do the same to the other two cups and the three plates.

3. Cut the ribbon into two equal lengths.

4. Holding the ends together, thread them through the hole in one cup, as shown below.

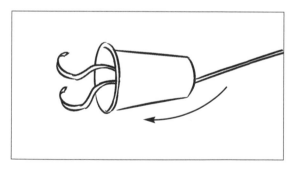

5. Thread the ribbons through the top of the small plate and then through the bottom of the second cup.

6. Now, thread the ribbons through the top of the other small plate and then through the bottom of the last cup.

7. Thread both the ribbon ends through the top of the large plate and secure the ends to the bottom of the final plate with sticky tape, as shown below.

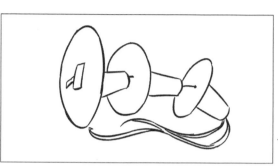

8. Hold the ends of the ribbon on to the first cup in one hand and sit the cake stand down on its base with the other hand. Carefully, tie the ribbon ends in a knot and finish with a bow.

9. Arrange the cupcakes on the cake stand.

Now all you need to do is plan the perfect tea party. Turn the page to find out how.

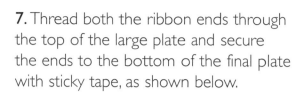

SUMMER PARTY PLANS

Throwing a tea party takes planning. Follow the advice below
to ensure your party day runs perfectly.

Send invitations. Choose some friends to invite to your tea party. Decide when and where you plan to hold the party and then fill in the invitations on the opposite page. Cut each one out and colour them in before handing them out to your friends.

Choose a menu. As well as baking cute cupcakes to serve (see pages 14 to 15), traditional tea-time foods also include dainty sandwiches, scones with jam, and cream cakes.

Choose a colour scheme. Choose two colours that go well together – for example, pink and blue or yellow and green. Pick a tablecloth to match your colour scheme and choose napkins in a contrasting colour.

Find flowers. Place a vase of flowers that work with your colour scheme in the centre of the table.

Be the hostess with the mostest. As your guests arrive, show them to the table and ask them to take a seat.

Tea alternative. Traditionally, people drink tea at tea parties. However, if you and your friends don't like the taste of tea, why not make a delicious 'watermelonade' drink? (See page 54 for a refreshing recipe.) Serve in pretty tea cups with matching saucers.

Once everyone has a drink and some food, take off your apron and join the party!

PRETTY PARTY INVITATIONS

Fill in the details on the invitation cards below, then carefully cut them out.

The letters RSVP appear at the bottom of each invitation – this is short for the French phrase 'répondez s'il vous plaît' which means 'please would you reply'.

Dear: ....
You are invited to a summer
tea party hosted by:

....

Location: ....
Date and Time: ....
RSVP

Dear: ....
You are invited to a summer
tea party hosted by:

....

Location: ....
Date and Time: ....
RSVP

Dear: ....
You are invited to a summer
tea party hosted by:

....

Location: ....
Date and Time: ....
RSVP

Dear: ....
You are invited to a summer
tea party hosted by:

....

Location: ....
Date and Time: ....
RSVP

Dear: ....
You are invited to a summer
tea party hosted by:

....

Location: ....
Date and Time: ....
RSVP

Dear: ....
You are invited to a summer
tea party hosted by:

....

Location: ....
Date and Time: ....
RSVP

Colour in each invitation before handing them
out to your friends.

What's being served at the teddy bears' picnic?

DID YOU KNOW?

One of these sizzling summer facts is not true.
Can you guess which one?

FACT 1. The hottest place ever recorded on Earth was El Azizia in Libya. On 13th September 1922 the temperature reached 57.8 °C. Human muscles actually stop working at 50 °C, which makes it impossible to survive for long at these temperatures.

FACT 2. The world's most expensive ice-cream sundae is called the 'Frrrozen Haute Chocolate' and can be bought at the Serendipity 3 restaurant in New York. It costs $25,000 (£15,000) and is served with a golden spoon.

FACT 3. In many countries Midsummer's Day is traditionally celebrated with a bonfire that wards away evil spirits. According to ancient tradition, the healing power of herbs is strongest on this day, especially if picked at sunrise. Healers and witches would set out before dawn to gather herbs to use for the rest of the year.

FACT 4. Wearing dark colours keeps you cool. This is because light colours absorb heat, whereas dark colours reflect it.

FACT 5. In the part of Finland that is in the Arctic Circle, the sun doesn't set for 73 days during the summer.

FACT 6. The end of summer and not getting enough sunshine can cause an illness called 'SAD' (Seasonal Affective Disorder). It makes you feel tired and moody, and is treated with bright lights.

FACT 7. In 1952, a group of friends had a very unusual barbecue on a six-metre long grill. They cooked a fully-grown crocodile that had eaten an antelope. The antelope roasted inside the crocodile's stomach, and the friends enjoyed a mixed-meat feast served up with fresh mango.

KITE CONFUSION

Six pieces from this jigsaw have got mixed up with some pieces from another jigsaw. Can you find the six pieces needed to go in the gaps?

PERSEPHONE'S PROBLEM

'Come on Artemis. Keep up!' shouted Persephone as she sat laughing in the sunny meadow. Just as Artemis threw herself down next to her friend, the ground next to them opened up and flames leapt up out of the hole. The girls screamed in terror as a man appeared in the flames.

'I am Hades,' he bellowed, 'God of the Underworld.' He grabbed Persephone's arm and pulled her through the flames into the hole in the ground. They had disappeared into the Underworld!

When Artemis told Persephone's mother, the goddess of harvests and farming, what had happened, the sun hid behind black clouds, the birds stopped singing and the leaves fell from the trees. 'Without Persephone, there can be no summer!' she cried. And sure enough, as weeks passed and Persephone could not be found, a winter frost covered the ground.

Persephone's mother visited Zeus, King of the Gods, and begged him to help her. 'Your daughter is in the Underworld,' replied Zeus. 'She can only return if no food has touched her lips since she has been there.'

Meanwhile, in the Underworld, Hades had fallen in love with Persephone. He presented her with a fruit called a pomegranate. Persephone had not seen the sun for many weeks, and the fruit reminded her of summer. She put six of the seeds into her mouth, and they were the most delicious things she had ever eaten.

Eventually, Zeus decided that Persephone could return to her mother. However, because she had eaten the six pomegranate seeds and had broken his rule, she would have to spend six months of every year living in the Underworld with Hades.

Artemis was overjoyed to see her friend when she came back and Persephone's mother was so happy that the ice melted and summer returned. But each year when Persephone had to go back to the Underworld, winter would once again descend.

PERSEPHONE'S PINK POMEGRANATE PUDDING

Pomegranate seeds look like beautiful pink jewels, and you can buy this delicious fruit in most supermarkets and greengrocers.

To make a pretty pink pomegranate pudding that'll bring the feeling of summer into your dining room, follow the steps below.

You will need: (this recipe serves 4)

- 1 ripe pomegranate • a large pot of plain yogurt
- 9 shortbread biscuits • some fresh mint leaves

1. Place eight of your shortbread biscuits in a plastic food bag. Use the end of a rolling pin to bash them into small pieces.

2. Remove the biscuit crumbs from the plastic bag and divide them between four glass tumblers.

3. Cut the pomegranate into quarters and place in a large bowl of water.

4. Keeping the pomegranate below the surface of the water, use your fingers to remove all the seeds. The seeds will sink to the bottom and any white pith will float to the top.

5. Remove the pith from the top of the water with your hands, then use a sieve to drain the seeds.

6. Empty the yogurt into a mixing bowl and add the pomegranate seeds. Use a metal spoon to mix them together, and watch as the yogurt turns pink.

7. Spoon the pink yogurt mixture into each of the tumblers.

8. Crumble some of the extra shortbread biscuit on top of the pudding and decorate with a few fresh mint leaves. Serve with a spoon. Yum!

SECRET SAFARI

You're visiting a safari park, but where are all the animals?

Below is a map of the safari park. To read it you will need to use coordinates. A coordinate is a letter and a number that refers to a location on a map. To use a coordinate, place your finger on the letter on the left-hand side of the map. Trace your finger along the row to the column that matches the number. In that square you will find the animal that the coordinate refers to.

Can you work out which animals live at the following coordinates?
Check your answers on page 62.

1. D3 **2.** B1 **3.** F3 **4.** C6 **5.** A4 **6.** E6

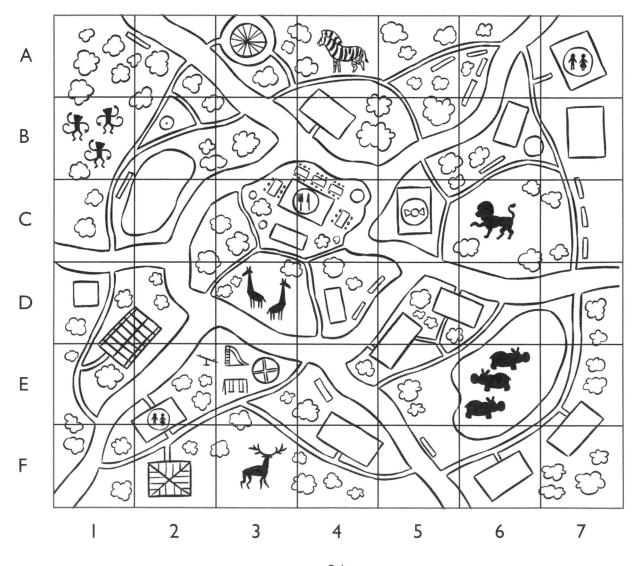

WHAT'S YOUR SUMMER STYLE?

Answer A, B, C or D to the questions below, then find out which summer style suits you best on the next page.

1. Your friend turns up at your house unexpectedly. What are you wearing?

A. A tracksuit and trainers

B. A spa-style dressing gown

C. Your new dress

D. A pair of customized jeans

2. What is your favourite way to spend a summer afternoon?

A. Playing frisbee in the park

B. Relaxing on a sun-lounger

C. Going for a picnic with a friend

D. Working on a craft project

3. What is your favourite summer breakfast?

A. Scrambled eggs and orange juice

B. Yogurt with fruit and honey

C. Croissants with butter and jam

D. Home-made muesli

4. Which of the following best describes your ideal perfume?

A. Fresh and fruity

B. Deep and musky

C. The newest one in the shop

D. A mixture of your favourite essential oils

5. What kind of bag do you pack for a sleepover?

A. Your gym bag

B. An oversized beach bag

C. A small, stylish suitcase

D. The bag you made last weekend

6. What is your summer hairstyle?

A. A ponytail

B. A glamorous blow-dry

C. You like to change your hairstyle regularly

D. Accessorized hairstyle with lots of grips/hairbands etc

WHAT YOUR ANSWERS MEAN

Count up how many of each letter you have chosen. Now look below to work out what your answers say about your style. If you scored an even mix of letters, this means you have a totally unique summer style – you go girl!

MOSTLY A:
SPORTS SUPERSTAR

You're an active girl who's always bursting with energy. You like to spend time outside and love meeting up with your friends to play team games. You're super-fit and always have a healthy glow. Why not turn to pages 12 and 13 to find out how to make up your own street-dance routine?

MOSTLY B:
GORGEOUS GODDESS

For you, the summer holidays are all about taking time out to pamper yourself. Your bedroom could compete with any of the top spas. You feel comfortable in any clothes – as long as your hair and skin are looking good you don't care! Turn to pages 8 and 9 for some summery beauty tips.

MOSTLY C:
FASHIONABLE FRIEND

You love flicking through fashion magazines, and your friends look to you as someone who is always ahead of the latest trend. Turn to pages 32 and 33 to learn how to hold a Summer Swap Shop party.

MOSTLY D:
CREATIVE KITTEN

You're an arty girl who likes to dress differently to your friends. You're brilliant at making the latest fashions your own and use the summer holidays to put your ideas into practice. Turn to pages 52 and 53 for a creative project that will last you all summer.

WACKY WINDOW WELLIES

Brighten up your windowsill with these wacky Wellington-boot plant pots.

You will need:

• acrylic paints (or a selection of nail varnishes in different shades will do) • paintbrushes • a pair of old wellies • a metal corkscrew • some soil and gravel from the garden or local garden centre • a selection of seeds or plants

1. Paint a design of your choice directly on to both boots. (Always rinse out your brushes with water when you have finished painting.)

2. Ask an adult to pierce a small hole through the sole of each boot, using a corkscrew. This hole allows excess water to drain out of your wellies.

3. Pour a cup of gravel into each boot and then fill up to the top with soil.

4. Bury some seeds just under the surface of the soil and pour some water over it. Place the boots on a small plate to catch any excess water, then pop on a sunny windowsill.

5. Water your wellies once a week, or if it's really hot, every other day.

WHAT SHALL YOUR GARDEN GROW?

Here are some ideas to get you started:

• Herbs and edible plants: cress, mustard or mint
• Pretty flowers: sunflowers, marigolds or pansies
• Fragrant flowers: lavender or sweet peas.

Top Tip. Plant ready-grown flowers rather than seeds for instantly pretty pots.

CINEMA RACERS

It's Friday afternoon and the school bell has just rung. Race your friends through the park to get to the cinema in time for the start of the film.

Place a coin for each player in the start box then take it in turns to spin the spinner (follow the instructions opposite to find out how) and move forward the number of spaces shown.

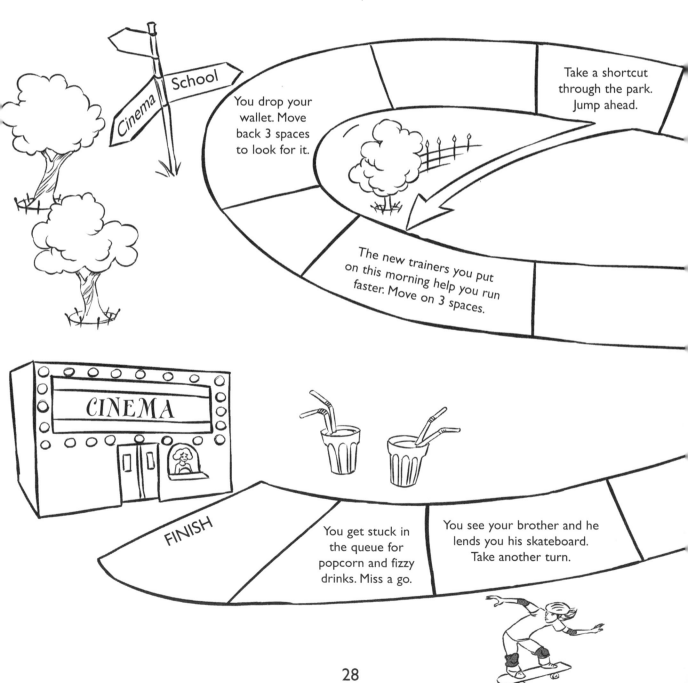

Cinema   School

Take a shortcut through the park. Jump ahead.

You drop your wallet. Move back 3 spaces to look for it.

The new trainers you put on this morning help you run faster. Move on 3 spaces.

CINEMA

FINISH

You get stuck in the queue for popcorn and fizzy drinks. Miss a go.

You see your brother and he lends you his skateboard. Take another turn.

SCHOOL

START

SPINNER

1 2 3 4 5 6

Cut out this spinner and pierce a toothpick through the centre.

To spin your spinner, hold the toothpick on your playing surface and spin it between your thumb and forefinger. When it stops spinning, the number at the top of the spinner is the number of spaces you should move your coin.

You left your bag at school and had to go back and get it. Miss a turn.

There's a kitten stuck in a tree. Miss a turn while you get it down.

Use the bridge to cross over the park lake. Jump ahead.

You see a cute puppy and stop to say hello. Miss a turn.

The sun is shining on you! Spin again to take another turn.

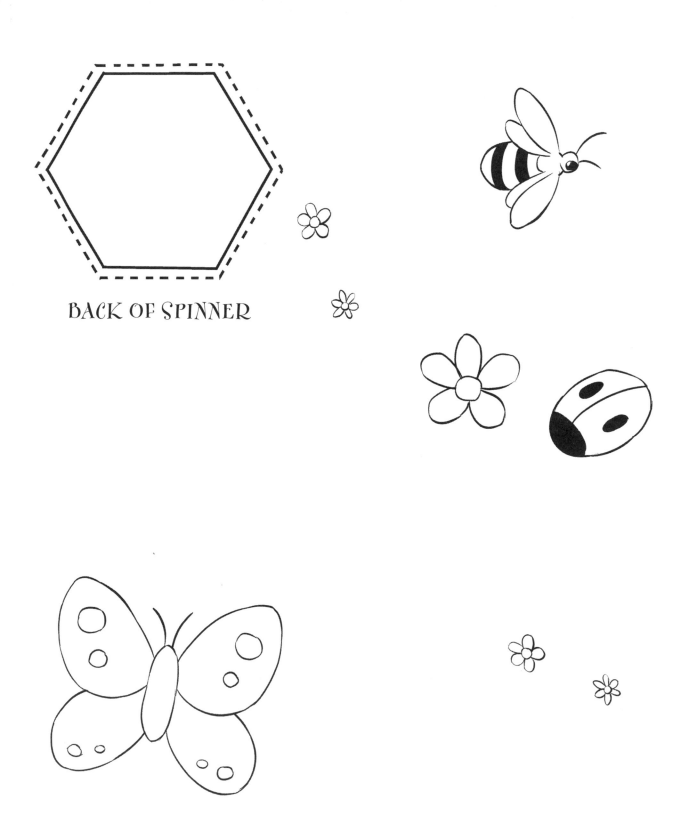

BACK OF SPINNER

Fill the page with flowers, butterflies, bees and ladybirds.

30

PURR-FECT PETS

You're visiting a friend who has lots of pets. How many of each type of animal can you spot? Check your answers on page 62.

Dogs	
Rabbits	
Cats	
Birds	
Hamsters	
Fish	
Snakes	

SUMMER SWAP SHOP

If you're bored of your clothes and have a wardrobe full of items that you don't wear anymore, why not host a Summer Swap Shop? Follow the steps below and see what new sassy style you end up with.

1. Choose a date for your Summer Swap Shop party and invite your friends around to your house.

2. Ask each friend to bring any clothes, shoes or accessories that they don't wear anymore, and would be happy to swap for something new.

3. On the day of the Swap Shop, designate areas of a room for different items – these might include skirts, tops, dresses, hats, belts, scarves etc.

4. Cut out a differently coloured square of paper for each of the designated areas. Stick a coloured square to the floor, table or chair, next to each area that you have designated.

5. As your guests arrive, ask them to place their items of clothing in the correct areas.

6. Write the name of each guest on to a differently coloured square of paper – according to which item of clothing that they brought to the party. For example, if skirts are in the red area, write the guest's name that brought a skirt on a red square.

7. Put all of the squares with names on into a large bowl and mix them up. Take it in turns to pull a ticket out of the bowl. The guest named on the ticket can then choose an item of clothing from the appropriately coloured pile.

PLAY THE 'STEAL THAT STYLE' GAME

Read on for a different swapping game called 'Steal That Style'. This is a fun game to play at a Summer Swap Shop – the aim is to decide who gets to keep what.

1. Put all the clothes in the middle of the floor.

2. Each player must then choose one of the styles listed below, or think of one of their own.

Boho-Chic   High-street Cool   Sari Sensation

Beach Babe   Sophisticated Sister   Emo

3. Two players then have one minute to look through all the clothes and accessories on display and put together an outfit in the chosen style.

4. The two players then model their outfits. Why not clear a catwalk down the centre of the room for them to walk down like models?

5. The other players then vote for which of the models has done the best job of recreating the style. The model who wins gets to keep one item from their outfit.

6. Repeat with other players and other styles. Happy swapping!

FASHION FRENZY

Backstage at a fashion show things aren't going well.
Can you solve the problems and help the show run smoothly?
Check your answers on page 63.

MODEL MATCH

These models are meant to be walking down the catwalk with dogs in their handbags, but their bags have all been muddled up. Follow the leads to find out which bag belongs to which model.

These models are due on the catwalk in three minutes – can you help them find their missing shoes to complete the matching pairs? Which poor model doesn't have a matching pair?

MAKE-UP MAYHEM

The make-up artist has just had a tantrum and quit! Quick, use colouring pencils to give these models makeovers that match the theme of their shows.

Hollywood Glamour

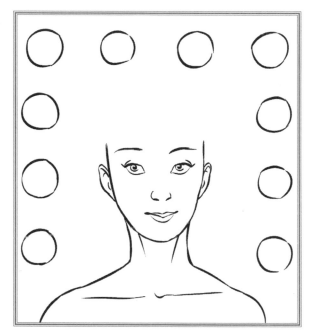

8os Retro

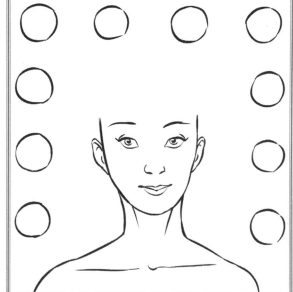

Vampire Chic

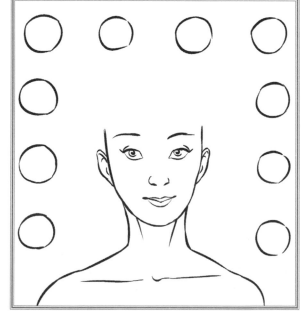

Natural Beauty

ALL THE FUN OF THE FAIR

Roll up, roll up! Turn your living room into a fairground with these fun fête games, then invite your friends to come and play.

ROLL UP FOR THE RAFFLE

1. Find three items that you don't mind giving up as prizes for your raffle, such as a teddy bear, a chocolate bar and a funky headband.

2. Write the numbers '103', '107' and '115' on a piece of paper and cut them out. Use sticky tape to stick them to your prizes.

3. Fold a piece of A4 paper in half four times, then unfold it so that you can see the rectangular fold lines. Starting at 100, write a number in each of the rectangles, as shown until you reach 115. Cut along the fold lines and fold each rectangle in half. Place all the folded pieces of paper into a bowl.

100	101	102	103
104	105	106	107
108	109	110	111
112	113	114	115

4. To enter the raffle, each player must choose a piece of paper from the bowl. If the number matches one of the numbers stuck to a prize, the player wins that prize.

BEST ANIMAL IN SHOW

Ask your guests to bring their best animal cuddly toy to the fair, and explain why their toy is the best, including any special tricks they can perform. Each guest has to give each (animal) marks out of ten for appearance, special features and lovability. Whichever animal has scored the most points wins 'best in show'.

SPLAT THE RAT!

1. Make a 'rat' by cutting the feet off an old pair of nylon tights and stuffing one foot inside the other. Tie up at the top with string. Use felt-tip pens to draw eyes, nose and whiskers on to the stuffed part.

Make sure your rat is small enough to easily slide through a cardboard tube from inside a roll of wrapping paper.

2. Use sticky tape to attach the cardboard tube to a large piece of card.

3. Use felt-tip pens to write 'Splat The Rat' on to the card, then use lots of sticky tack to fix the card to the wall. The bottom of the tube should be just below your knee.

4. Each player must be given a kitchen roll tube to use as a bat. Drop the rat through long the tube for the player to try to hit the rat with the bat before it reaches the floor.

BOWLING SOCK BALLS

1. Line up a collection of seven clean empty yogurt pots upside down on the floor. Write a number from one to seven on a piece of paper and cut out each number. Pop a number randomly under each yogurt pot.

2. Place a piece of A4 paper on the floor about two metres away from the pots. Roll up a pair of socks into a ball.

3. Players must then take it in turns to roll the sock-ball across the floor to knock over as many yogurt pots as possible. Count up the points from inside each yogurt pot the player knocked over and write down their score. The person with the most points is the winner.

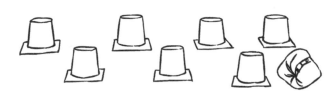

Draw the missing girls standing in front of these body-bending mirrors.

GET YOUR SKATES ON

These identical twins are out rollerskating together. Can you spot ten differences between them? Check your answers on page 63.

Draw more trees in the park.

SUMMER BY THE SEA

Complete these seaside-themed puzzles and turn to page 63 to check your answers.

Which four of the details below are from the picture of the rockpool?

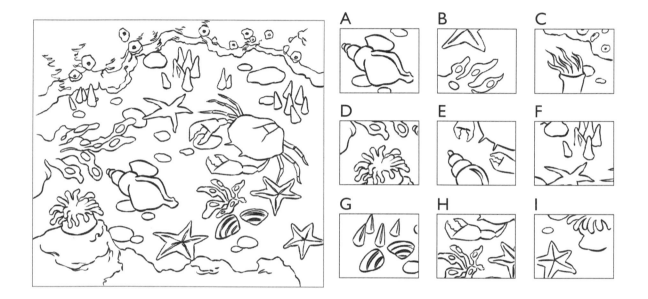

Which two of these ice-cream sundaes are identical?

Look at these beach volleyball players.

A. How many of the players are wearing shorts?

B. How many have at least one arm in the air?

C. How many are wearing flip-flops?

D. How many are wearing sunglasses?

Design daring sails for these boats.

SUMMER SCIENCE

Turn your house into a laboratory with these exciting experiments.

HOW TO BRING A PAPER FISH TO LIFE

'Surface tension' is a property of all liquids. It is a bit like a layer of skin on top of the liquid. It is the reason that water collects in droplets and why small insects can walk on the surface of lakes and rivers. Carry out this science experiment to see the effects of surface tension in action.

Start by cutting out some fish from paper – trace the template of the fish opposite to make each one. Next, fill a washing-up bowl with water and place the paper fish flat on the surface.

Take a bottle of washing-up liquid and squeeze a small drop behind the tail of each fish. The soap will break the surface tension of the water, causing the fish to swim away at speed.

HOW TO MAKE A RAINBOW

Sunlight is made up of all the colours of the rainbow, and when it passes through water it splits up into light waves of different lengths, which we see as different colours. You can catch these light waves by standing a mirror in a saucer of water, on a table in front of a window.

Wait for a day when the sun is streaming through your windows for this experiment. Move the mirror around until the light passes through the water and bounces off the mirror, making a rainbow appear on the wall.

HOW TO MAKE A RAISIN DANCE

Prepare this experiment by filling a glass with water, and another glass with lemonade. Ask a friend what they think will happen when you drop a few raisins into the glass of water. She will probably guess correctly that the raisins will fall to the bottom. This is because objects sink when they are more dense than the liquid they're in.

Now ask your friend what they think will happen when you drop a few raisins into the lemonade. She will probably guess that the raisins will sink or float, but in fact they'll dance up and down in the lemonade for about an hour!

This is because of the bubbles of gas that make the lemonade fizzy. They attach themselves to sides of each raisin as it sinks to the bottom of the glass. When enough gas bubbles are attached to a raisin, it begins to float up to the surface again. When each raisin reaches the surface of the lemonade, the bubbles pop and cause the raisin to sink, until it becomes light enough to float again.

HOW TO MAKE YOUR EARS RING

The sound a guitar makes occurs because the vibration of the strings makes sound waves. You can create your own sound waves that will travel directly along a piece of string into your ears. All you need is a fork, a spoon and a long piece of string.

Tie the fork to the centre of the string, and tie one end of the string to your left index finger, and the other end of the string to your right index finger. Put one finger on each ear and let the fork dangle down.

Ask a friend to tap the fork with the spoon. The sound will travel up the string causing a loud ringing sound in your ears.

GO GREEN

Saving energy on your summer holiday will help save the planet.

Read the facts below to find out how you can go green on holiday, then follow the doodle instructions to make the house planet-friendly.

GREEN GUIDES

• Ask an adult to unplug electrical appliances when you leave home to save energy. Never leave them on standby (with a red light shining) as this uses up energy.

• Find out where the local bike-hire shop is and get cycling. Riding a bike is much better for the environment than using a car.

• Go green at the supermarket by encouraging your parents to only buy locally grown fruit and veg – not items that have been flown around the world. When you get home, why not grow you own fruit and veg in your garden or in a window box?

Fill the vegetable patch with home-grown veg.

Give her bike wheels so it's ready to ride.

• Save water by turning the taps off while you brush your teeth. Don't do any laundry on holiday – wait until you get home to do one big wash to save water.

• Recycling bottles, cans, paper and cardboard will mean your waste gets turned into something else, which saves energy. Ask at the local tourist information office to find out where the recycling bins are located.

Draw the TV. Make sure it is turned off.

Draw the curtains to let natural light in and save electricity.

Fill the washing machine with your holiday washing.

Fill the recycling bin with bottles, paper and cans.

FUN ON THE FARM

There's lots going on down on the farm in the summertime.
Complete these farmyard puzzles, then check your answers on
pages 63 and 64.

How many birds and how many apples can you spot in the orchard?

Can you spot five differences between the two horses with their foals?

Can you help the dog find his way home through the woods?

These cows are jealous of their stylish friend. Give them a similar splodgy pattern.

SUMMER SPINNERS

Liven up your garden or window box with these
special summer spinners.

You will need:

• three pieces of plain paper • a drawing pin
• a pencil with a rubber on the end • scissors • a glue stick • felt-tip pens

1. Trace the pattern below on to two pieces of paper.

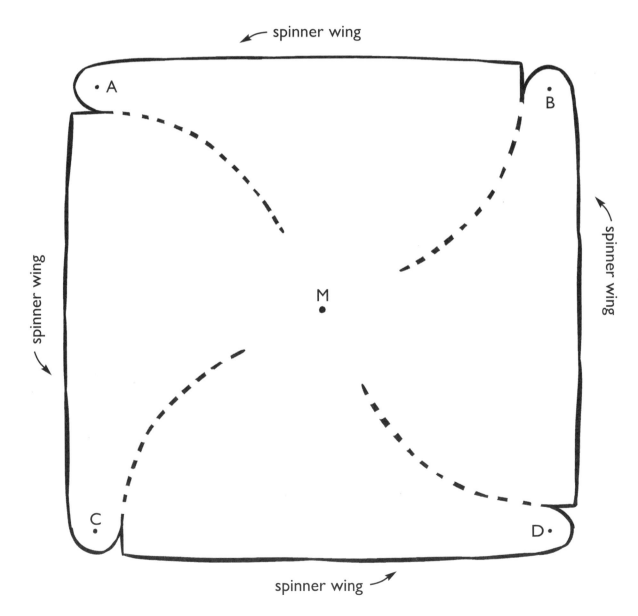

spinner wing

spinner wing

spinner wing

spinner wing

A

B

C

D

M

2. Carefully cut out each pattern along the solid lines.

3. Line up the two shapes so that they fit nicely back-to-back. Glue them together.

4. Using your felt-tip pens, doodle a different design on each side of the spinner shape – why not draw flowers and spots on one side and cherries and stripes on the other?

5. Trace the star shape below on to the third piece of paper.

Draw a dot in the middle of the star. Colour in the star shape and cut it out.

6. Carefully cut along the four dotted lines of the spinner shape.

7. Fold the corners of the spinner wings (the areas labelled **A**, **B**, **C** and **D**) into the middle of the spinner shape (**M**).

8. Use the drawing pin to carefully poke a hole through the dot in the centre of the star. Now pierce a hole through each of the spinner wings – each wing should now be pinned behind the star.

9. Carefully push the end of the pin into the side of the rubber on the end of the pencil.

10. Place on your windowsill or in your garden on a breezy summer's day and watch it spin and make pretty patterns.

Decorate these summer spinners.

GARDEN GAMES

The girls are having plenty of fun in the sun in the garden scene below.
Why not join in the fun and have a go at completing these puzzles?
All the answers are on page 64.

Using only three straight lines, divide the garden scene below so that there
are only two girls in each section.

Can you spot the following animals and insects in the garden scene above?

• 11 birds • 7 butterflies • 5 cats • 7 ladybirds • 3 mice

Fill the page with summer fruits.

SEW ... FANTASTIC!

The long summer holidays are the perfect opportunity to get creative.

Add colour and texture to your bedroom with a range of scatter cushions made from different fabrics. Here's how to make your own.

For each cushion you will need:

- an old cushion • a length of fabric (big enough to wrap around the cushion)
- thread in a colour that matches your fabric • a needle • scissors • sewing pins
- beads, buttons and so on to decorate • old newspaper • 2 lengths of ribbon

1. Cut out a piece of fabric that is roughly twice the size of the cushion, leaving an extra 5 cm of width around the edges.

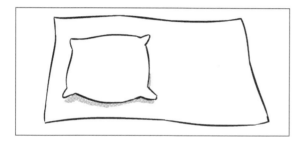

2. Fold the fabric in half, as shown below.

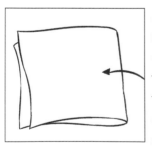

3. Fix sewing pins along the outside edges of the fabric to hold it together. Leave one side of your square unpinned.

4. Thread your needle using roughly 1½ m of thread. Tie a double knot in the end of it. Push the needle through one corner, closest to the fold of the cushion cover. Pull through on the other side of the knot.

5. Pull the needle back through the fabric about 1½ cm ahead of your original point and again, gently pull the thread through.

Once you have done this, push the needle back through the fabric in the same point that you started. Pull the thread through. Now push the needle through the fabric again, roughly 1 cm ahead of the last point, as shown below.

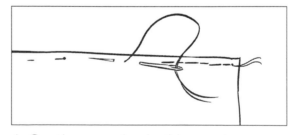

6. Continue sewing in this way in a straight line until you are about 1½ cm from the next corner.

7. Rotate the fabric a quarter turn and sew along the next edge as you did in step **5.**

8. When you reach the next corner of the cushion cover, secure your stitches by sewing over the same spot ten times. Cut off any excess thread.

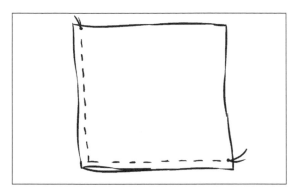

9. Turn the cushion cover right side out and place a piece of newspaper inside it – this will stop you sewing through both sides of the fabric in the next step.

10. Decorate one side of the cushion cover by stitching on buttons, beads, sequins and coloured feathers to create your own design. Remove the newspaper when you are done.

11. Insert the old cushion inside the cover along the open end.

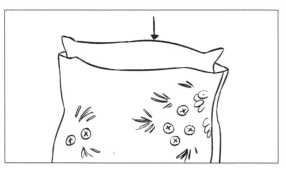

12. Carefully use the scissors to make two snips in the top layer of fabric. The snips should divide the open end into thirds, and be about 2 cm from the edge of the fabric. Make identical snips in the same places on the bottom layer of fabric.

13. Use the lengths of ribbon to close the cushion by tying the top layer of fabric to the bottom layer. Secure with a bow.

14. Make as many cushions as you like and scatter them over your bed, or give as presents to your friends and family.

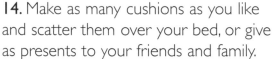

STAY COOL

When the temperature rises, keep your cool with these top tips.

HOT HEAD

If your head's cool the rest of your body will be too. To cool down, simply dip a headscarf in cold water then wring it out so that it's damp, but not dripping. Wrap it over your head and tie in a pretty bow at the base of your neck.

WATERMELONADE

This delicious watermelon lemonade is perfect for cooling yourself down on a hot day. Cut slices of watermelon, remove the peel and pick out the seeds. Blend in a food processor – ask an adult to help you with this.

Press the pulped watermelon through a strainer into a large jug. Add lemonade and mix together with a whisk. Garnish with slices of watermelon and a sprig of mint.

FRUITY CUBES

Fill an ice tray with water. Cut pieces of lemon and lime and place one in each cube. Carefully slide the tray into your freezer and leave for a couple of hours. Add to summer drinks for a cool citrus chill.

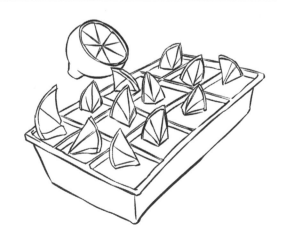

OCEAN SPRAY

Find an empty bottle with a spray function – hair products and suntan lotions often come in this kind of bottle. Thoroughly wash the bottle so that there's none of the old product left inside.

Fill the bottle with water and squirt a little of your favourite perfume into the bottle. Keep it in the fridge and use it to have a quick refreshing spray after being outdoors.

FAN-TASTIC

Draw a pretty pattern on a piece of A4 paper. Pleat the paper by folding every two centimetres, as shown below.

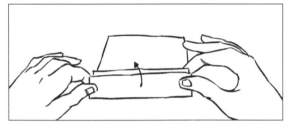

Take two lollipop sticks and glue one to each end of the paper so that the top of each stick is in line with the top of the paper. Tie a piece of ribbon around the bottom of the paper to create a handle.

WATER COOLER

Keep bottles of drinking water in the freezer and take one with you when you're going out to play in the sunshine. The ice will gradually melt, giving you a supply of cool, refreshing water.

If you are hot when you go to bed at night, pop a bottle of frozen water in front of a fan. The chilled air will get pushed around the room and cool you down.

SUMMER MAGIC

Add a bit of magic to your summer with these brilliant tricks.

HOW TO SAW A LADY IN HALF

Fool your friends into thinking you are cutting a lady in half … luckily she is made of paper so, if anything does go wrong, no one gets hurt!

You will need:

• paper • pen • envelope • scissors

1. To prepare this trick, first seal the envelope shut then cut off the ends to create a tube shape.

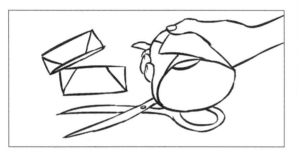

2. Flatten out the tube again, so that the top and bottom of the envelope meet in the middle. Cut two slits from the new edge up to just before the central crease. The slits should separate the tube into thirds.

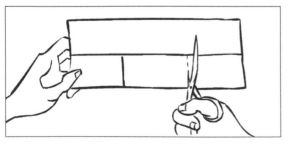

3. Cut a strip of paper, roughly 10 cm wide and about 5 cm longer than the length of your flattened tube shape.

4. Draw a picture of a lady on to the piece of paper, like this:

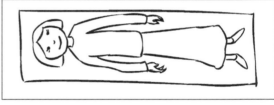

5. Re-shape the flattened tube so that it forms a tube shape again. Position it in the palm of your hand so that the slits are at the back.

6. Slide the paper lady (picture side facing upwards) inside the tube shape, pushing her feet through the first slit so that they come out of the back of the envelope, and then bring her feet back inside the tube by pushing them through the second slit. The back of the tube shape should now look like this:

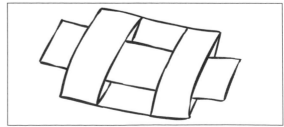

7. To perform the trick, cut the tube in half, making sure that your scissors cut through the middle of the tube – being careful to cut above the paper lady.

8. Finally, pull the lady out from the two pieces of envelope, and amaze your audience when she appears unharmed!

HOW TO CHANGE A BALLOON'S COLOUR

Learn how to make a balloon magically change colour … just by popping it!

You will need:

• a green balloon • a yellow balloon • sticky tape • a pencil • a pin

1. Before performing this trick, you will need to first make a double-sided loop of sticky tape. Stick it on to the middle of the yellow balloon.

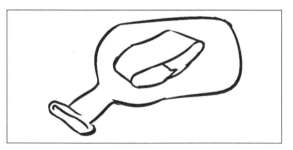

2. Push the unsharpened end of a pencil into the yellow balloon's neck. Then, push the same end into the green balloon. Slide it down until it is completely inside the green balloon.

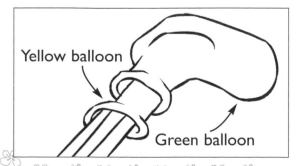

Yellow balloon

Green balloon

3. Blow up the yellow balloon (which will also blow up the green balloon outside it) and tie a knot in the bottom of both balloon necks.

4. Now stand in front of your audience, holding what they will think is a blown up green balloon.

5. Locate where the sticky tape is on the yellow balloon by looking through the green balloon on the outside. Jab a pin in here.

The green balloon will burst, revealing the yellow balloon inside it. It will look like the balloon has magically changed colour!

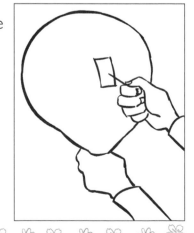

Doodle the magical land through the wardrobe.

THE STRANGE CASE OF THE ISLAND CAVE BEAST

'I made a new friend at the beach today,' announced Lily to her sister, Kate. 'I fell over in a rockpool and a girl called Cat got some ice for me to put on my knee. She lives here on the island and she won the 'Young Surfer Of The Year' award this summer.'

'Hey, there she is!' exclaimed Lily as they rounded a corner. Kate looked in the direction her sister was pointing, but all she saw was a flash of grey.

'What on earth was that?' cried Lily, her heart pounding in her chest. Cat had disappeared and in her place was what looked like a huge animal that scampered off down the hill. 'Oh no!' exclaimed Kate. 'You don't think that was the Cave Beast do you?'

'I thought that was just something written in the guidebook to scare us,' said Kate, her voice shaking as she spoke. According to island legend, the Cave Beast was a fearsome creature that lived in an underground cave, but no one knew if it was real or not. 'It certainly did look like some kind of beast … and here's some grey fur caught on the wall.'

Lily felt a lump form in her throat. 'We've got to find her!' she exclaimed. 'I can see some more fur caught over there. Quick, they went this way.' The girls ran down the hill and stopped at the entrance to a cave. Lily was standing frozen looking into the entrance of the cave. Just inside was the red towel that Cat had been carrying earlier that day.

'We have to save her!' Lily grabbed hold of Kate's hand and pulled her into the cave. There was a long, dark tunnel ahead. As they approached the end, bright daylight momentarily blinded the girls, and their ears rang with the sound of children's voices. They were bewildered and frightened, but as their vision returned to normal they hugged each other in delight. 'It's a theme park!' exclaimed Kate.

'And there's Cat,' cried Lily. She rushed towards her. 'Cat!' she called. 'We saw you disappear with a giant animal and we thought you'd been captured by the Cave Beast!'

Cat laughed. 'This is the Island Theme Park, and that was just my friend Daniel. Here he is now.' Lily and Kate couldn't stop giggling as they were introduced to Daniel, who was dressed in a grey, furry animal suit.

'I can get you in for free,' Daniel offered. 'There's a Cave Beast ride I think you might enjoy!'

HOME SWEET HOME

Summer holidays are perfect for enjoying time at home. So pop your slippers on and settle down to these homey puzzles. All the answers are on page 64.

SUDO-COOK

Complete this sudoku grid, so that the four different kitchen items shown below – the oven glove, the spoon, the saucepan and the mixing bowl – appear only once in each column, each row, and in each of the four larger squares.

TIME FOR TEA

Can you match the teacups to their saucers below in time for tea?

BUNKBED MADNESS

Four sleepy girls want to go to bed. Can you find which bunk belongs to which girl?

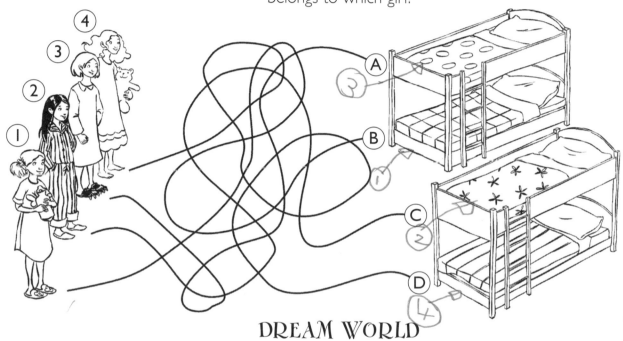

DREAM WORLD

You dream you are lost in a strange house. Can you find your way through the maze of corridors to your bedroom?

ALL THE ANSWERS

SUMMER SNAPS
PAGE 5

1. E, 2. D, 3. A,
4. B, 5. F, 6. C

DID YOU KNOW?
PAGE 20

FACT 4 is wrong. Wearing light colours actually keeps you cool on a sunny day. Dark colours absorb heat, whereas light colours reflect it.

SECRET SAFARI
PAGE 24

1. Giraffes
2. Monkeys
3. Deer
4. Lion
5. Zebra
6. Hippos

KITE CONFUSION
PAGE 21

PURR-FECT PETS
PAGE 31

○ 4 dogs
⬠ 3 rabbits
△ 4 cats
◇ 1 bird
☆ 5 hamsters
⬡ 3 fish
♡ 1 snake

FASHION FRENZY
PAGE 34

Model **A** has dog **5**.
Model **B** has dog **4**.
Model **C** has dog **2**.
Model **D** has dog **1**.
Model **E** has dog **3**.

Model **C** doesn't have a matching pair.

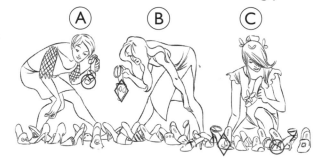

GET YOUR SKATES ON
PAGE 39

SUMMER BY THE SEA
PAGES 40 AND 41

Squares **A**, **D**, **F** and **H**.

A. Six, **B**. Five,
C. Seven, **D**. Zero.

FUN ON THE FARM
PAGES 46 AND 47

17 apples and 12 birds.

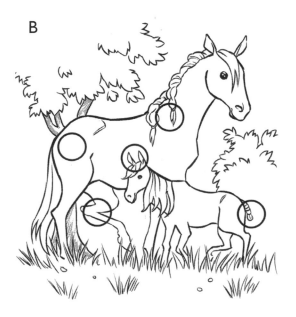

HOME SWEET HOME
PAGES 60 AND 61

GARDEN GAMES
PAGE 50

○ 11 birds

◇ 7 butterflies

⬠ 5 cats

△ 7 ladybirds

⬡ 3 mice

Girl **1** has bed **B**.
Girl **2** has bed **C**.
Girl **3** has bed **A**.
Girl **4** has bed **D**.